SENSES

TOUCH

Anita Ganeri

W
FRANKLIN WATTS
LONDON • SYDNEY

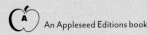 An Appleseed Editions book

Paperback edition 2017
First published in 2015 by Franklin Watts

© 2012 Appleseed Editions

Created by Appleseed Editions Ltd,
Well House, Friars Hill, Guestling,
East Sussex TN35 4ET

Designed and illustrated by Guy Callaby
Edited by Mary-Jane Wilkins

A CIP record for this book is available from the British Library

ISBN 978-1-4451-3253-2

Dewey Classification: 612.8'8

Picture acknowledgements
l = left, r = right, c = centre, t = top, b = bottom
page 1 GekaSkr/Shutterstock; 2 iStockphoto/Thinkstock;
3t Hemera/Thinkstock; c iStockphoto/Thinkstock;
b wavebreakmedia ltd/Shutterstock; 4 mojito.mak.gmail.com/
Shutterstock; 6l Minerva Studio/Shutterstock; r iStockphoto/
Thinkstock; 7tr karam Miri/Shutterstock; tr Brand X Pictures/
Thinkstock; bl and br iStockphoto/Thinkstock; 8 MaszaS/
Shutterstock; 9t Photodisc/Thinkstock; b Hemera/Thinkstock;
10 iStockphoto/Thinkstock; 13 Hemera/Thinkstock;
14 iStockphoto/Thinkstock; 15 Hemera/Thinkstock;
16 Suzanne Tucker/Shutterstock; 17 Werner Heiber/
Shutterstock; 18 Photodisc/Thinkstock; 19 Stockbyte/
Thinkstock; 20 Dmitriy Shironosov/Shutterstock; 21t Hemera/
Thinkstock; 21 Hemera Technologies/Thinkstock; 22t PRILL
Mediendesign und Fotografie/Shutterstock; l Anton Prado
PHOTO/Shutterstock; r Milos Luzanin/Shutterstock;
b Jaroma/Shutterstock; 23t iStockphoto/Thinkstock;
b Aaron Amat/Shutterstock; image beneath folios holbox/
Shutterstock
Cover: iStockphoto/Thinkstock

Printed in China

 MIX
Paper from
responsible sources
FSC® C104740
www.fsc.org

Franklin Watts
An imprint of Hachette Children's Group
Part of The Watts Publishing Group
Carmelite House
50 Victoria Embankment
London EC4Y 0DZ

An Hachette UK Company
www.hachette.co.uk

www.franklinwatts.co.uk

Contents

Touchy, feely

What happens when you stroke a cat? What does it *feel* like?

Does the cat's fur feel soft and silky, or hard and rough?

4

Touch is one of your senses. Your senses tell you about the world around you.

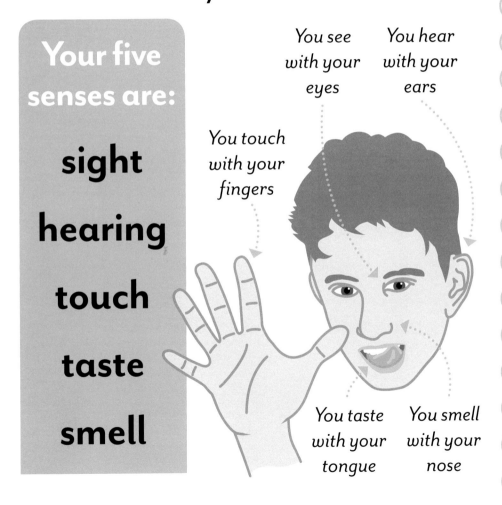

Your five senses are:

sight

hearing

touch

taste

smell

You see with your eyes

You hear with your ears

You touch with your fingers

You taste with your tongue

You smell with your nose

What can you touch?

Your sense of touch tells you how things feel. You can feel whether things are rough or smooth.

You can feel whether something is hard or soft. You can feel whether something is hot or cold.

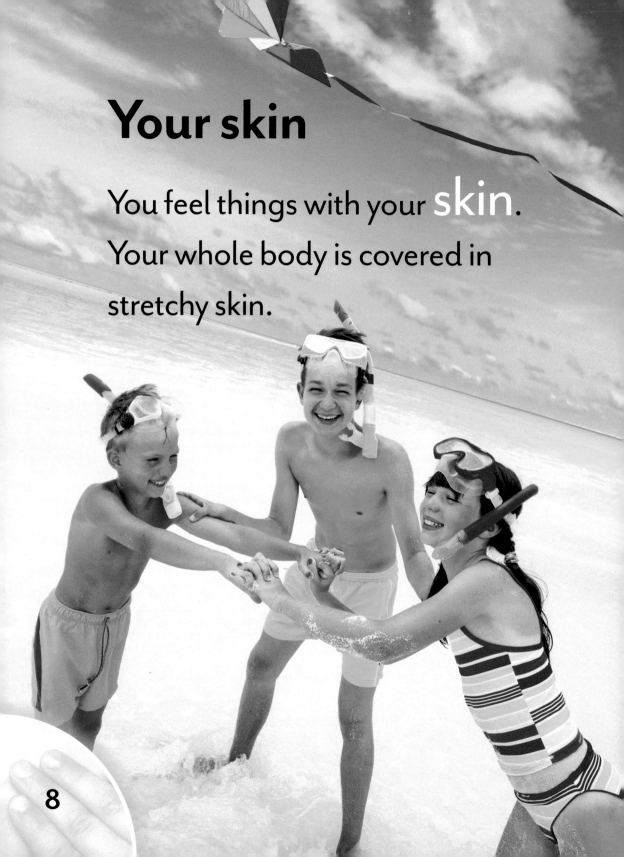

Your skin

You feel things with your skin.
Your whole body is covered in
stretchy skin.

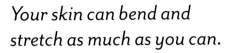

Your skin can bend and stretch as much as you can.

Your skin holds your body together. It bends and stretches as you move about.

In most places, your skin is only as thick as **cardboard**.

Under your skin

Your skin has two layers.
The top layer gets worn out, but
new skin quickly grows again.

The skin on your hands has ridges to help you grip.

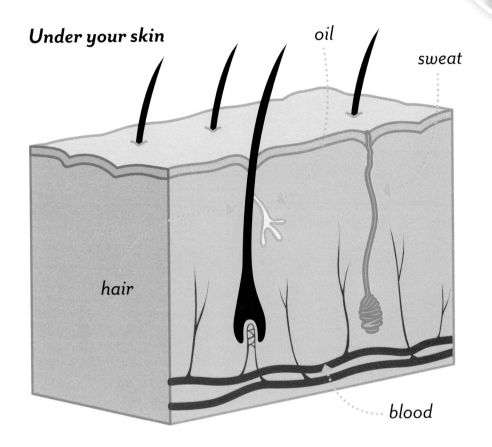

Under your skin

oil

sweat

hair

blood

Lots of things happen under your skin. Tiny tubes carry blood. Other parts make oil and sweat.

Touch messages

There are also millions of tiny **nerves** under your skin. Each kind feels a different thing.

Nerves under your skin

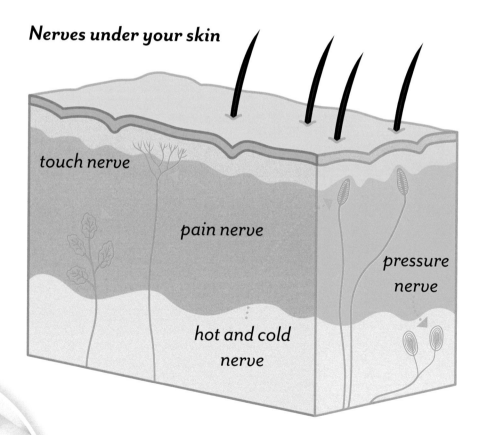

touch nerve

pain nerve

pressure nerve

hot and cold nerve

Then the nerves send messages to your brain to tell you what you can touch and feel.

Sensitive skin

Some parts of your skin are more sensitive than others because they have more nerves.

The skin on your toes has lots of nerves in it.

The skin on your fingertips, lips and toes is the most sensitive. The skin on your back and bottom is the toughest.

Painful touch

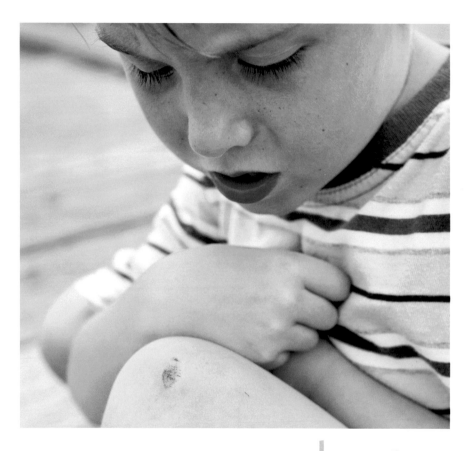

Grazing your knee can hurt a lot. But pain can be a very useful feeling, too.

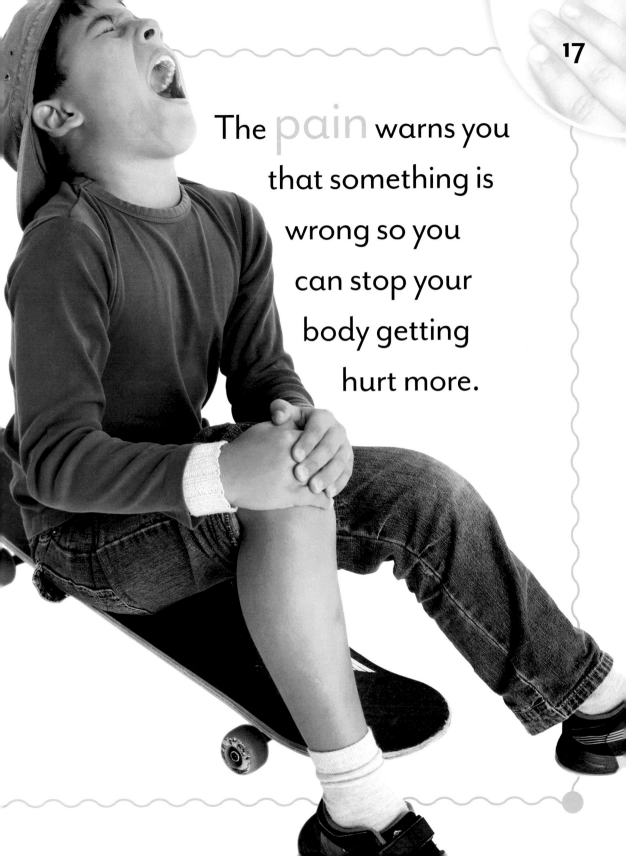

The pain warns you that something is wrong so you can stop your body getting hurt more.

Useful skin

Your skin does lots of other useful jobs. It stops your insides getting harmed. It is also **waterproof**.

Your skin quickly
mends itself if
you cut yourself.
It makes a scab
until new skin grows.

Hair and nails

Hair grows out of tiny holes in your skin. Hair grows on your body and head.

What colour hair do you have?

You have about **five million** hairs on your body and head.

Nails also grow from your skin.
They are useful if you have an itch!

Touch facts

The patterns on the skin on your fingertips are called your fingerprints. No one else has the same fingerprints as you.

The dust in your house is mostly made up of dead skin cells. You lose millions of these every day.

Blind people can read books by passing their fingers over patterns of bumps, called Braille.

On average, the skin of a rhinoceros is about five centimetres thick; ten times thicker than yours.

Useful words

nerves
Thin, long wires inside your body that carry messages between your body and brain.

scab
A hard patch of dry blood that forms over a cut in your skin.

sensitive
How much or how little different parts of your skin can feel.

sweat
Watery liquid that oozes from tiny holes in your skin. It helps to cool down your body.

Index